The Question & Answer Book

ALL ABOUT STARS

ALL ABOUT STARS

By Lawrence Jefferies
Illustrated by Joseph Veno

Troll Associates

Library of Congress Cataloging in Publication Data

Jefferies, Lawrence.
    All about stars.

    (The Question and answer book)
    Summary: Answers such questions as ''What is a star?'',
''Why do stars twinkle?'', and ''How long does a star live?''
    1. Stars—Juvenile literature. [1. Stars—Miscellanea.
2. Questions and answers] I. Veno, Joseph, ill.
II. Title. III. Series.
QB801.7.J43 1983   523.8   82-20027
ISBN 0-89375-888-4
ISBN 0-89375-889-2 (pbk.)

What do you see?

Look up at the sky on any clear night. You'll see hundreds of stars shining brightly. Maybe you'll see a shooting star streak across the sky. Or, if you look closely, perhaps you'll see how certain groups of stars seem to form pictures in the dark sky. The universe of stars is a beautiful sight.

What *is* a star?

A star is a gigantic ball of glowing gas. But stars are so far away that they look like tiny, twinkling points of light.

Without a telescope, you can only see a few thousand stars in the night sky. But with a telescope, you can see many more stars. The lens at the far end of a telescope is like a magnifying glass. It makes faraway objects look bigger. Even with a small telescope, you can see hundreds of thousands of stars.

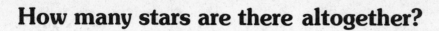

How many stars are there altogether?

Astronomers—scientists who study the stars—say the number of stars in the universe is about 200 quintillion (200 billion billion). That's 200 followed by 18 zeroes.

Most stars are so far away that you cannot see them at all. Among the stars you *do* see, there is one you will never see at night. Do you know which star it is?

It's the sun. When the part of the earth we live on turns away from the sun, the sun's light does not reach us. It is nighttime, and we don't see the sun—until the next morning. Of all the stars, the sun is the closest to us. Because it is near us, it *seems* to be the brightest and biggest star in the sky. But it isn't. It is really only a medium-sized star.

The North Star is the most famous
star in the sky. When you point to it,
you are pointing north.

Here is how you can find the North Star.

First, find the Big Dipper. The Big Dipper is a group
of stars shaped like a dipper, or long-handled drinking
cup. Find the two stars at the end of the cup of the Big
Dipper. They point straight to the North Star. The
North Star is always in the same place in the sky—it is
directly over the North Pole. That is why it is so
important. It shows where north is. Once you know
where north is, you can find other directions, like east
and west, without a compass. Many sailors in ancient
times used the North Star to find their way safely
across the ocean.

What is a constellation?

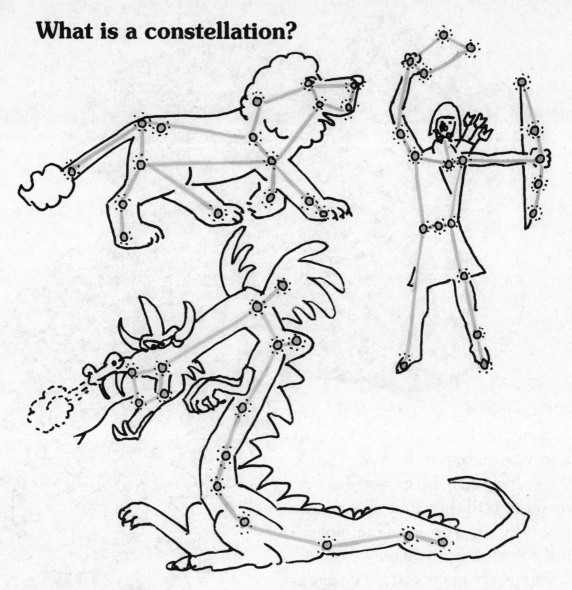

The Big Dipper is a *constellation*. A constellation is a group of neighboring stars that look like a giant picture in the sky. Long ago, people thought that each constellation looked like a certain person or animal or thing. That's why we have constellations with names like Orion the Hunter, the Dragon, and the Lion.

On some evenings, just as the sky darkens, you may see what looks like a wonderful star in the west. This is the *evening star*. Except for the moon, it is the brightest object in the night sky. And on some mornings, just before dawn, you may see the *morning star* in the east. Long ago, people thought these were two separate stars, but they were wrong. These "stars" are not stars at all. They are actually planets. At certain times of the year, Venus is both the evening star and the morning star. At other times, the planet Mercury is the morning and evening star.

What is a shooting star?

On hot August nights, you might see a long streak of light called a *shooting star*. Shooting stars are not really stars. They are chunks of rock falling through the earth's air. As they fall, they heat up and glow. Astronomers call these trails of fire *meteors*.

Some of the stars you see are really twins. They are *double stars*. Did you ever watch a car come toward you on a dark night? You probably saw a single light at first—when the car was far away. Then, as the car came closer, you could see two separate headlights. Double stars are like headlights that are far away. They are so close together that they look like a single star. Double stars are also called *binary stars*. The middle star in the handle of the Big Dipper is really two stars, close together. It is a binary star.

Stars are different colors.

Stars are colorful. A star's color depends on its temperature. Cool stars are red. Warmer stars—like the sun—are yellow-orange. Hot stars are white. Very hot stars are blue.

The brightest stars are also the best-known ones. Sirius, rising on cold winter nights, is the brightest star in the night sky. The next brightest stars are Canopus, Alpha Centauri, Arcturus, and Vega.

Did you ever wonder where stars go in the daytime?

Actually, they don't go anywhere. They are still right there, shining in the sky. But in the daytime, the light from the sun is so bright that you cannot see the light coming from the other stars.

In the evening, just as it starts to get dark, try an experiment. Lie on your back and look up at the sky. As the sunlight fades, you'll see the stars "pop out," almost one by one.

Why do stars twinkle?

Astronomers are not really sure. They think it is because the earth's air is moving. As light from the stars passes through the moving air, the stars look as if they are twinkling. If you were on the moon and looked at the stars, they would not twinkle, for there is no air on the moon.

The Milky Way

On a clear night, when the moon is not in view, you may see a white band of light stretching across the sky. It is straight above you. This is called the *Milky Way*.

The Milky Way is a *galaxy*—it is *our* galaxy. A galaxy is made up of dust, gas, and many stars. Seen from far away, each galaxy forms a special shape in space. The Milky Way contains billions of stars and is shaped like a giant pinwheel. From the earth, we cannot see the pinwheel shape. Since the earth is a part of the galaxy, we can only see the edge of the pinwheel. To us, our galaxy looks like a milky band in the sky.

Some other galaxies are also shaped like pinwheels. But you can only see their pinwheel shapes when they are seen through a big telescope. Galaxies may have other shapes, too. Some are round. Others are shaped like a football. All contain billions of stars.

How many galaxies are there?

There are several billion galaxies in the universe. In the Northern Hemisphere—the half of the earth north of the equator—you can see only one other galaxy besides the Milky Way with your naked eye. It is located in the constellation called Andromeda, and it is called the Great Spiral in Andromeda. The Great Spiral is a pinwheel-shaped galaxy like our Milky Way.

In the Southern Hemisphere, two other galaxies can be seen without a telescope. They look like two large clouds and are called the Magellanic Clouds. These galaxies were named after the explorer Ferdinand Magellan. He was one of the first navigators to observe them.

What is a nebula?

Far out in space are giant clouds of gas and dust. They are called *nebulas*. Some nebulas have stars in them. The most famous nebula is the Sword of Orion. It is in the constellation of Orion the Hunter.

NEBULA

SWORD

Some nebulas are dark, because they have no stars to light them up. Dark nebulas often appear as dark clouds when they are seen through a big telescope. From the Southern Hemisphere, people can see a famous dark nebula called the Coalsack. It is near the constellation called the Southern Cross.

What is a nova?

Sometimes a new star seems to appear in the sky. It is called a *nova*. *Nova* is the Latin word for "new," but this kind of star is not really new. It is an old, dim star that suddenly explodes and becomes very bright. A nova may stay bright for a few days, weeks, or even months. Then it fades out of sight.

Every so often a star explodes *very* violently. It becomes extremely bright. It is called a *supernova*. A supernova is one of the most exciting events in astronomy.

The Crab Nebula is a famous supernova. It is not really a nebula, but a large star that exploded. The Crab Nebula was once so bright it could even be seen in the daytime. Now it has grown much dimmer, and can only be seen with a telescope. There is a simple reason why this supernova is called a crab—it looks like one. It is in the constellation of Taurus, the Bull.

How far away are the stars?

When astronomers use miles or kilometers to measure distances in space, they get numbers that are too big to use easily. For example, the nearest star to us, except for the sun, is Proxima Centauri. It is 26 trillion miles, or over 41 trillion kilometers, from the earth. A trillion has twelve zeroes.

When numbers are too big and clumsy to work with, scientists use a larger unit for measuring. In astronomy, they use a *light-year*. Like miles or kilometers, a light-year is a measure of distance. A light-year is the distance that a beam of light travels in one year. It is almost 6 trillion miles (10 trillion kilometers).

How far away is Proxima Centauri? It is a little more than 4 light-years away from the earth.

How big are the stars?

Some stars are big. Some are middle-sized. Others are small.

The biggest stars are called *supergiants*. They are more than a thousand times bigger than our sun. The star called Betelgeuse (pronounced "beetle juice"), which is located in the right shoulder of Orion the Hunter, is a supergiant.

Next in size are the *giant stars*. These stars are about one hundred times larger than our sun. Giant stars that are red in color are called *red giants*.

Most stars—about nine out of every ten—are about the same size as our sun. These are medium-sized stars.

The smallest stars are called *dwarfs.* They are only about half the size of the earth—some are even smaller. Some dwarfs shine with a very white light. They are called *white dwarfs.* One of the smallest stars known is a white dwarf. It is called Van Naamen's Star.

Life of a star

In a way, stars are like people. Stars are born. They grow up. They grow old. They die.

Stars are born in clouds of gas and dust. The gas is mainly hydrogen. Tiny particles of hydrogen gas and dust begin whirling together. As they bunch together, they attract more and more particles. After a while, a huge ball of gas forms.

As the ball of gas grows larger, gravity pulls the gas and dust tighter together. The outer particles of gas press on the inner particles. This makes the inner particles get very hot. Things pressing on other things always make heat.

When the temperature is high enough, a *nuclear reaction* starts. Some of the hydrogen begins to change into a gas called helium. When this happens, a huge amount of energy is given off. Soon the nuclear reaction grows larger. The baby star starts to give off light and heat.

The center of the star becomes a gigantic furnace. It makes so much heat that the temperature there may be millions of degrees. The surface of the star is much cooler. At the surface, the heat goes off into space.

How long does a star live?

A star may live for thousands of millions of years. Our sun, for example, is already middle-aged. It is about 5 billion years old. It will probably live for another 5 billion years. Some stars, especially very large, hot ones, burn up quickly. They do not live as long as other stars do.

After a few billion years, a star like our sun starts growing old. It swells up into a giant star. Its surface cools off— and the star looks red. It is a red giant. Our sun may someday become a red giant.

Then the star will shrink and become much hotter—white-hot. The star may explode as a supernova. It may become a white dwarf. After billions of years, the white dwarf may cool down and die. That is what would probably happen if the star was about the same size as our sun when it was born. But if the star was a giant at birth, astronomers think it may die in a different way

As a giant star dies, it begins to shrink. It shrinks down to almost nothing. As it shrinks, its gravity increases. The force of gravity gets so strong that not even light can escape. The giant star is now a *black hole*. Anything that passes near it is pulled in. If a starship went near a black hole, it would probably disappear forever.

In the constellation of Cygnus, or the Swan, which you can see on summer nights, astronomers believe there is a black hole.

Do you know what some of the brightest objects in the sky are?

They are *quasars*. The word *quasar* means "star-like object." Quasars are so far away that they can only be seen with very strong telescopes. Astronomers do not know too much about them—except that they give off huge amounts of light. Some astronomers think that quasars may be the most distant objects in the universe.

Some stars are like giant radio stations. Such stars are called *radio stars* because they send out radio waves. Radio stars also give off lots of light—but most of these stars are too far away to be seen from earth. Many quasars are also radio stars. Astronomers can pick up the radio energy of stars with radio antennas. These antennas are shaped like giant bowls, and they are called *radio telescopes.*

Radio stars work something like lighthouses. In a lighthouse, a powerful light beam rotates, or spins. You see the light only when it shines in your direction. You do not see the light when it shines away from you.

Radio stars often have powerful radio beams. These stars also rotate. Astronomers notice these stars only when their radio beams point in the earth's direction. Their radio energy comes in *pulses*, or waves. That is why these stars are called *pulsars*. A star near the center of the Crab Nebula is a pulsar.

Is there life on other planets?

There are billions of billions of stars in the universe. Some scientists believe that most of the stars have planets moving around them. Could there be life in any of those distant solar systems?

So far, astronomers have not found signs of intelligent life anywhere else in the universe. But every day, they wait at their radio telescopes—hoping that a message will come through from somewhere out in space. They are searching for signs of life on other worlds.

Will they ever find it? What will it be like? Only time will tell.